CRAFT PROJECTS

PAPER & CARD

Erica Burt

Illustrated by
Malcolm S. Walker

Wayland

Craft Projects

CLAY
FABRICS AND YARNS
NATURAL MATERIALS
PAPER AND CARD
SCRAP MATERIALS
WOOD

First published in 1989 by
Wayland (Publishers) Ltd
61 Western Road, Hove
East Sussex BN3 1JD, England

Editor: Joan Walters
Designer: Kudos Services
Cover photograph by Paul Seheult

British Library Cataloguing in Publication Data
Burt, Erica
Paper and card - (Craft projects)
1. Handicrafts
I. Title II. Walker, Malcolm S. III Series
745.5
ISBN 1-85210-532-1

Printed in Italy by G.Canale & C.S.p.A., Turin
Bound in Belgium by Casterman S.A.

PAPER AND CARD

Contents

PAPER AND CARD

Introduction

Paper and card are used in vast amounts in today's busy world. They are not only used to write, print or paint on, but in wrapping and as containers and packaging. The Chinese were the first to make paper in 105 AD. Rags were washed and boiled and reduced to a soupy pulp. This was poured through a bamboo sieve. As the water seeped away a sheet of matted fibres was left. This sheet of paper was left to dry on a flat board. The Arabs brought paper-making to Europe, but it was not until 1840 that a German discovered a method of grinding logs into a fibrous pulp. Today paper is made from wood pulp. Different chemicals and size (glue) are added in varying amounts to produce different qualities of paper. China clay from Cornwall, Britain, is added to make heavy glossy papers. Card is made from a denser, thicker layer of wood pulp.

Here is a list of the equipment you will need to make the projects.

Papers
Sugar paper
Newspaper
Cartridge paper
Greaseproof paper
Tissue paper
Brown wrapping paper
Sweet papers
Doilies
Gummed paper
Wallpaper
Coloured mounting paper
Textured kitchen paper
Foil
Paper straws
Cellophane

Card
Corrugated card
Thin white card
Cardboard boxes
Cardboard tubes

Tools
Needle and thread
Scissors
Craft knife or blade
Metal rule
PVA glue
Coloured felt tips

This book will introduce you to the many different things you can do and make with paper. The project ideas will help you to think of your own creations. The projects are divided into what you can make by folding, curling, cutting or tearing. But once you start, you will want to combine these processes in your own ideas. Enjoy discovering and have fun making things with paper and card.

Safety rules and hints for working

1. Handle tools carefully to avoid accidents. Always ask an adult for help if you cannot do something on your own.
2. When cutting or scoring card always work on a board or on a thick pad of newspaper, so that you do not mark worktops.
3. Read through the whole of a project before starting it. You will probably think of alternative ways of creating. Each project will sow the seeds of an idea and it is much more fun for you to design your own individual creation.

PAPER AND CARD

Making paper

This project shows you how to make your own paper picture, or sheet of paper, using pieces of waste paper. Collect different kinds of paper such as wrapping paper, sweet papers, newspaper, computer paper, sugar paper, tissue paper, writing paper.

You will need

- Various kinds of paper, sorted into colours
- Simple frame (or sieve) about 12 cm x 20 cm covered with fine nylon curtain or similar material. A shoebox lid could be used by cutting away a rectangle.
- Bowls or large jars
- Blender (ask an adult first)
- Tray (or sink)

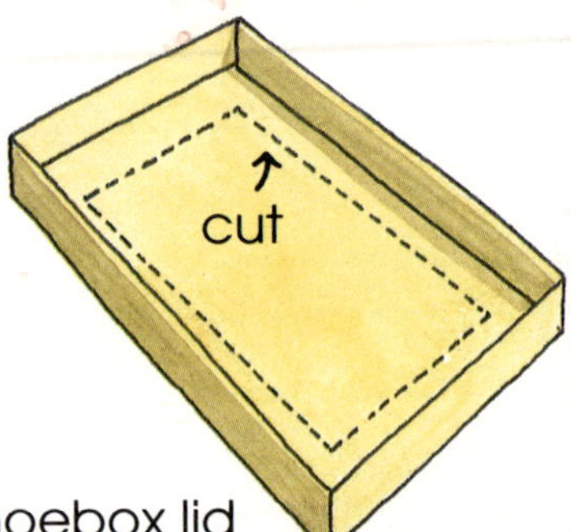

shoebox lid

Paper picture

1. Tear up your paper into small pieces.
2. Put into blender and add enough water to make a runny, sloppy pulp. (If you do not have a blender tear the pieces as small as you can.)
3. Put into jars or bowls, so that you have various colours of paper pulp.
4. Put wooden or card frame on to a tray or in a sink, so that the water from the pulp will drain through the gauze into it.

1 - 3

5. Using your fingers pick up chosen colour of pulp and place it on to the gauze frame to create a scene, or pattern.

6. The whole frame should be covered with paper pulp (any spaces will mean your picture will fall apart).

7. Twigs, flowers and grasses can then be added. A little pulp placed over the stalks will ensure they adhere properly.

6 and **7**

8. Leave the picture to dry out. (A pad of newspaper or tray will take up the excess water.)

9. After a day or so peel your paper picture off the frame.

More ideas

Make an island with paper pulp. Build up areas in relief to make hills. Add other natural materials to create a realistic scene.

By adding wallpaper paste and not making the pulp so watery, you can make papier mâché, a good material for modelling puppet heads.

PAPER AND CARD

Curling paper

You will need

- Coloured strips of paper (about 1 cm wide and 15 cm long)
- Knitting needle or pencil
- Sheet of card (A4 size)
- PVA glue

The art of curling paper is called quilling. It is a very old craft. Delicate designs and pictures were made by curling different coloured papers and setting them on their edges. Greetings cards were made using this technique.

Paper quilling

1. Wind a strip of paper round a knitting needle (or pencil) and let the coil slip off.
2. Stick the outer end to the coil.
3. Draw the outline of a picture or the letters of your name on to a piece of card.
4. Coat the coiled edge of the spiral with glue and press firmly into place.
5. The coil can be gently squashed into an oval, round or rectangular shape.

Paper curling

By curling paper round a pencil or pen, you can make attractive fringes for decorating paper or hair for masks. By curving card or paper into a cylinder, you can make the basis for a mask.

1 

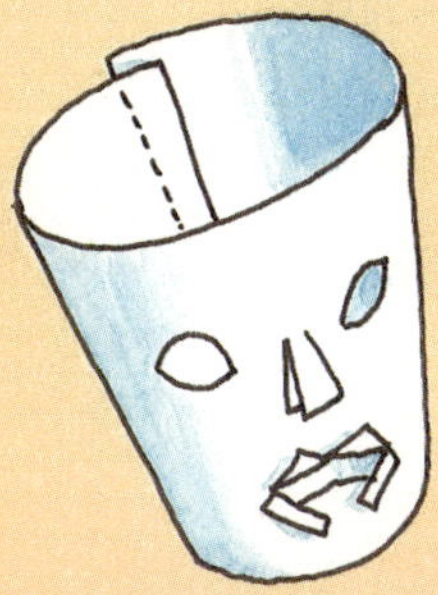 2

1. Draw a face on to paper or card.
2. Curve the paper or card into a cylinder and glue the ends together.
3. Curl strips of paper round a pencil or, using a single blade from a pair of scissors sharply stroke the length of a strip of paper - it will curl with the tension.
4. Stick the curls on to the cylinder to make hair, beards, moustaches, whiskers or feathers.
5. You can use your decorated cylinder as a mask by cutting holes for the eyes.

More ideas

Make a necklace or a bracelet by threading coils on to a thread.
Make different shaped coils in different colours. Some can be stretched out.

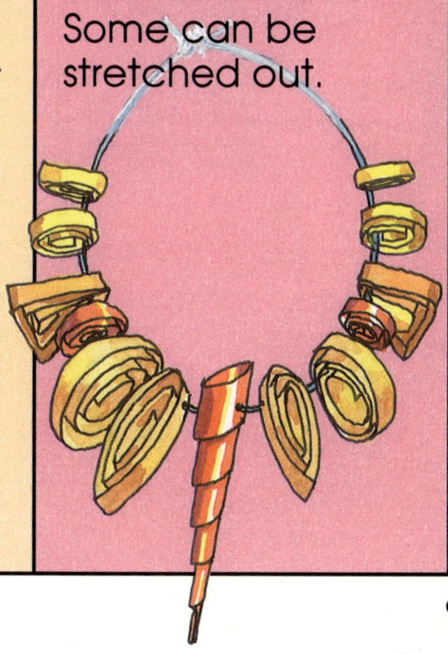

PAPER AND CARD

Folding paper

You will need

All you need are sheets of square paper (fold opposite corners) and some patience!

The ancient craft of folding a square of paper to create images is called origami. It originated in China and then found its way to Japan. It can become a fascinating hobby in itself. Here are plans which tell you how to make a frog and a cow.

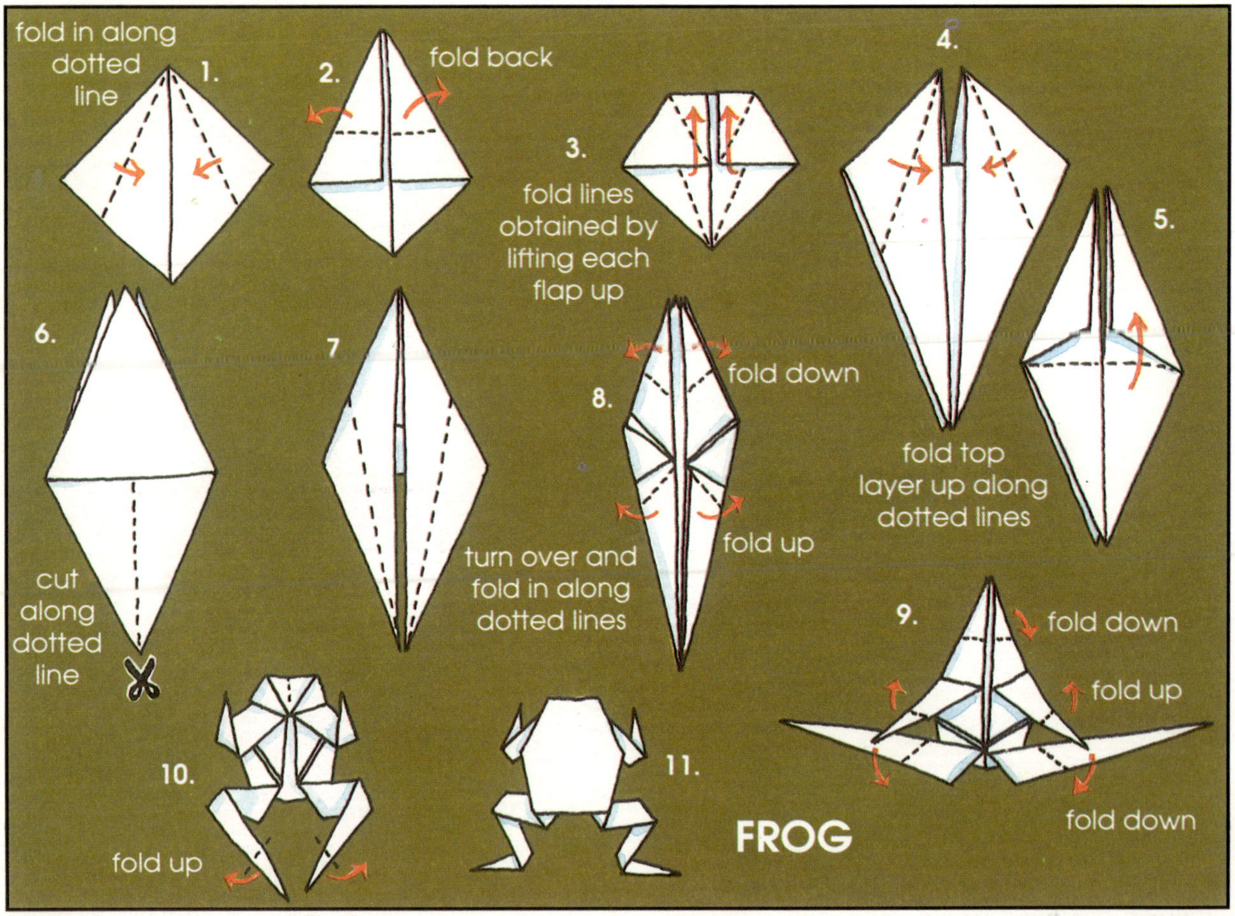

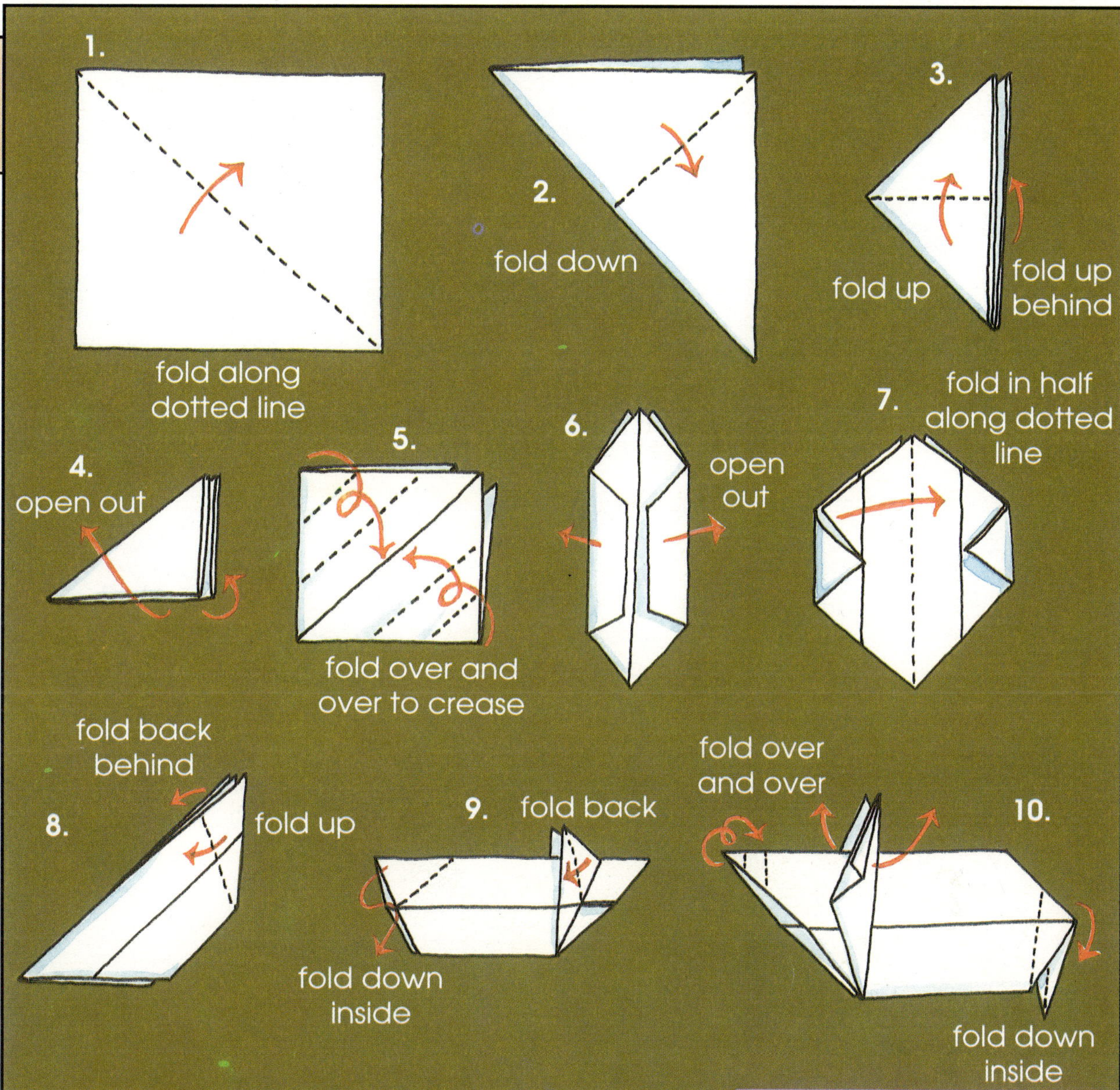

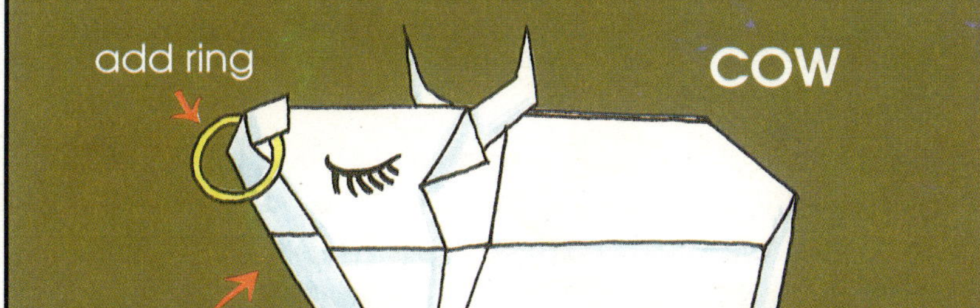

More ideas

Try and make your own folded animals and figures. Start with a piece of square paper.

PAPER AND CARD

Boxes and packages

You will need

- Thin white card
- PVA glue
- Scissors or craft blade
- Felt tips or crayons
- Pencil
- Ruler
- Needle and thread

More ideas

By not glueing the last surface of the cube you have a box that can hold a small gift - sweets, beads, a necklace, a handkerchief.

Using the template for a box, you can make various puzzles and games and many shapes for interesting packages.

Muddle cubes

1. Draw a cube on to the card, 8 cm square, following the template.
2. Provide tabs, as shown on the diagram, so that the box can be stuck together.
3. Cut out carefully, preferably using a craft blade.

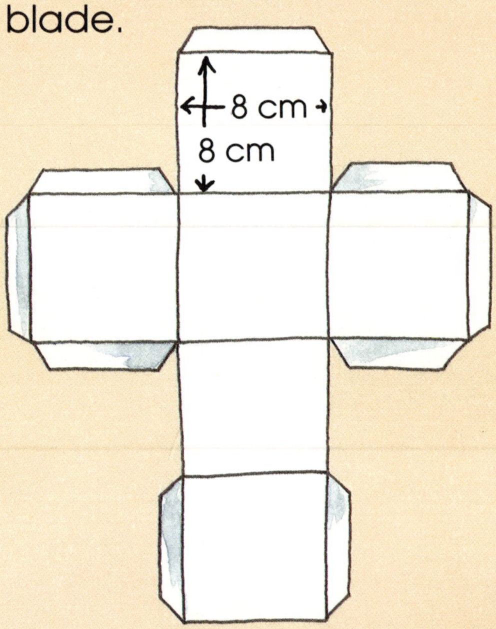

4. Draw and cut out two more templates the same size as the first one.

5. Place your three templates side by side. Carefully work out which surfaces are to be decorated with a similar design or pattern. You might choose to use letters and numbers. Why not make four figures that have to match? The top box has head and shoulders, the middle box arms and body, the bottom box the legs. If you make each figure very different from the other, you can get some amusing results.

6. Score fold lines.

7. Glue tabs and assemble cube, surface by surface.

8. Thread three boxes together with string or embroidery thread (you will need a needle at least 8 cm long).

Make a jack-in-the-box

Make a springy body by folding 2 strips of coloured paper over each other.

Stick one end to the inside of the box and stick the other end to a ping-pong ball with a face drawn on to it. You can make a figure out of a larger box. Make arms and legs out of springy strips and use curls of paper for hair.

Cutting paper

You will need

- Coloured paper
- Card
- Scissors with fine, pointed blades

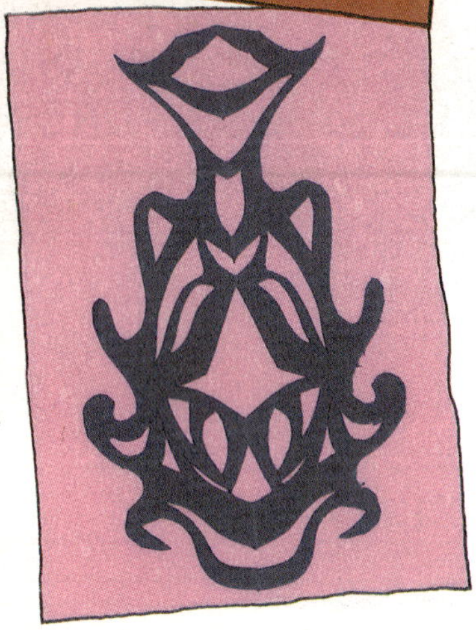

The Chinese cut very intricate designs in tissue paper and put them in their windows at festival times. The Polish have a special craft, called Wycinanki, where simple designs are cut freehand on folded paper. Beautiful patterns are the result. The paper can be folded more than once.

1. Fold a piece of coloured paper (about 14 cm x 11 cm) in half.
2. Draw a detailed pattern.

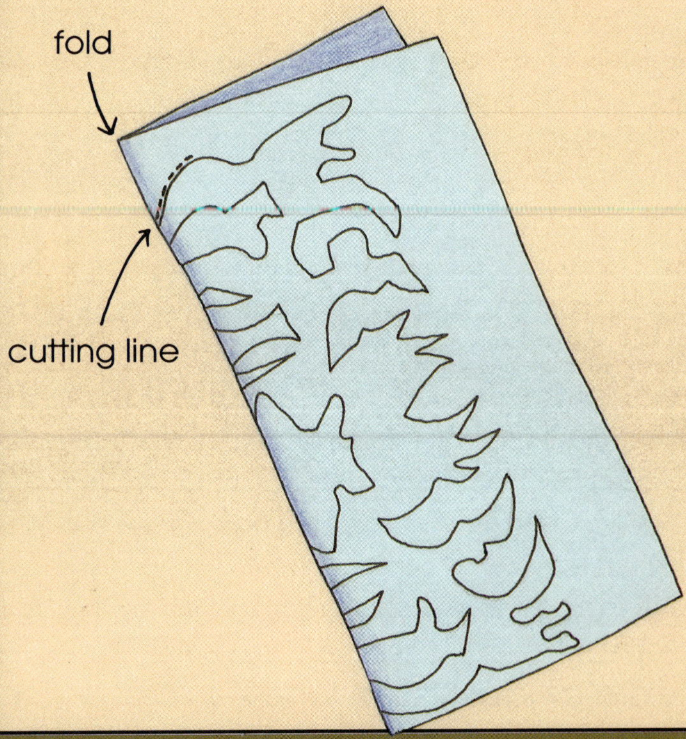

3. Cut carefully along lines drawn. Be careful not to cut away the length of the fold line.
4. The more intricate and detailed your cutting the more interesting your cut-out will be.
5. Unfold and stick on to a fold of card.

More ideas

Fold your paper twice again but remember not to cut away **all** the fold lines.

Use various colours of paper.

Superimpose one cut-out on top of another.

Make cards or designs as presents for friends.

PAPER AND CARD

Lampshades and masks

You will need

- Good quality cartridge paper or thin card
- Craft knife or scissors
- PVA glue

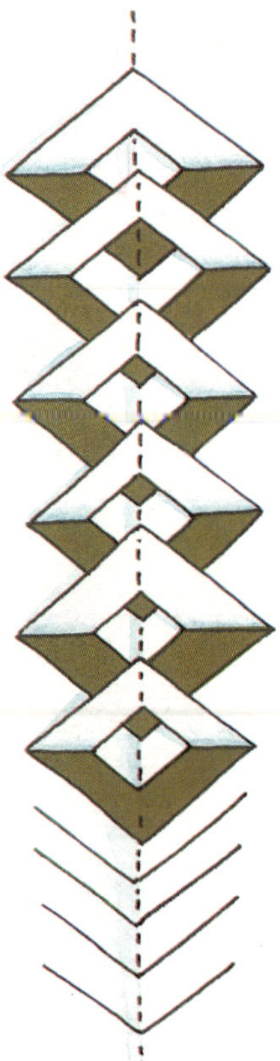

You can make very attractive lanterns or lampshades by carefully cutting patterns and holes into thick paper or thin card. Experiment first until you find designs that you like.

1. Take a sheet of paper and fold it like a screen, making the folds about 4 cm apart.
2. Make cut lines along each fold.
3. Open out and fold individual slots.

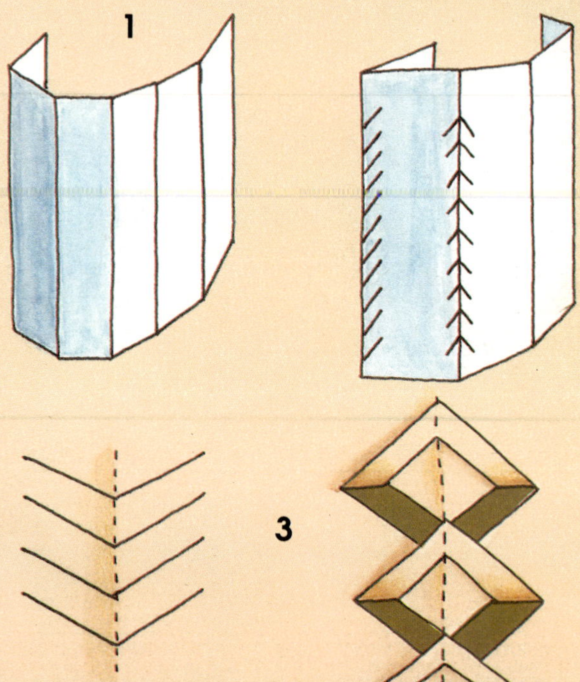

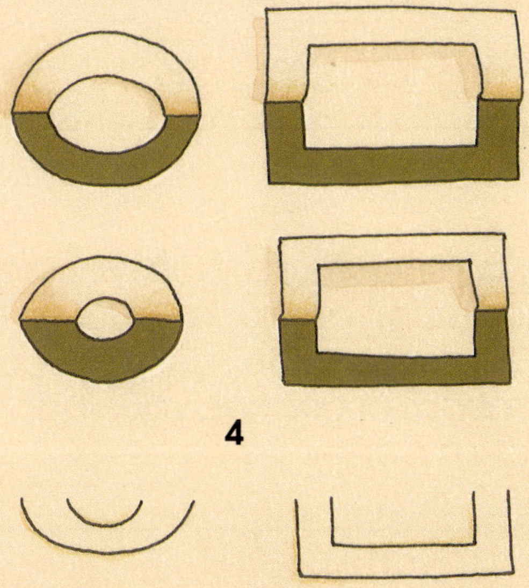

4. Repeat for each fold line.
5. Glue tab to make an attractive cylinder or lampshade.

More ideas

You can use these ideas to make an attractive mask.

Use a piece of card that is big enough to slip over your head once it has been glued to make a cylinder.

Add curls of paper for hair or make cuts in the card to create a fringe.

PAPER AND CARD

Cutting shapes

You will need

- Good quality card
- Scissors
- Sheets of paper on which to stick shapes
- PVA glue

By choosing your shapes carefully you can have fun producing animals, figures or possibly just a pleasing design. You can work in 3 dimensions or arrange your shapes flat on a sheet of paper.

1. Set yourself certain rules:

a) You must use all of your shapes
eg. 20 circles made up of
5 medium circles
5 small circles
10 large circles
or 25 identically sized triangles
or varied sized squares

b) They must/must not overlap.

c) How many ways can they be arranged to make a landscape or an animal?

2. When you have decided on your rules cut out the chosen shape and number.

3. Arrange and stick on to paper.

4. What can you make with a variety of shapes using only twelve pieces?

3-Dimensional construction

You do not have to use glue to make your construction. By making a slit into each piece of card you wish to join, you can make a suitably strong structure.

1. How big a standing construction can you make when all the shapes are circles.
2. Make a standing figure using a selection of shapes.
3. Using the template for the cube (page 12) make a pleasing construction of different sized boxes. Can you work out a template based on a triangle? By sticking the solid triangles together, you can make a pleasing construction.
4. Decorate different surfaces with felt tips or paints when you have made your structure.

More ideas

Make as many objects as you can using the Chinese **Tangram** design. Take a square of paper, divide it into the seven shapes shown on the diagram.

Cut out the shapes and have fun experimenting, making the shapes into pictures and patterns.

PAPER AND CARD

Making mobiles

Using coloured strips of paper and a simple motif or design, you can make a very attractive mobile for your room. If you do not want to weave paper, you can decorate a simple cut-out shape, or make simple cone figures. Remember to decorate both sides as both surfaces will be seen as they turn in the air.

You will need

- Sheets of paper
- Coloured paper strips or magazine pages
- Soft wire or thin cane
- Scissors or craft knife
- PVA glue
- Needle and thread

1. Weaving with paper

a)

Fold paper in half and cut along fold.

b)

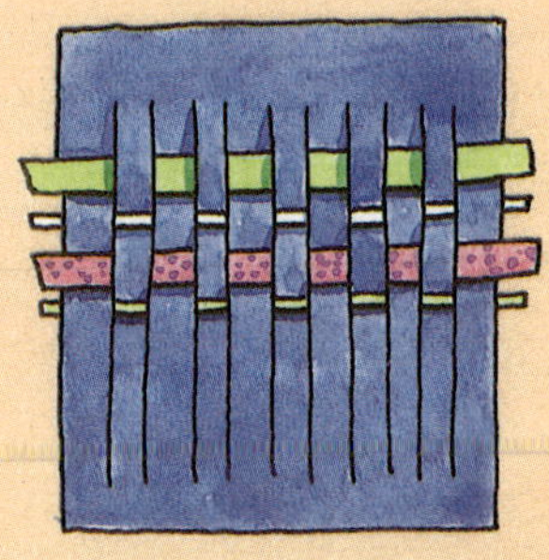

Weave thin strips of coloured paper in and out.

c) Cut out a simple shape.

Glue down ends at back of shape.

2. Decorate a simple shape with cut-outs

3. Cone figures

a) Cut out shape.

Lightly fold along dotted line.

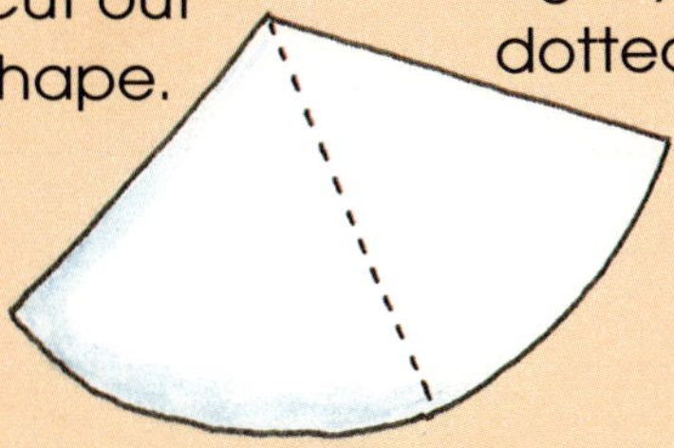

b) Stick on eyes and lips. Make cut along centre fold for nose.

c) Make eyebrows by fringing two small pieces of paper.

d) Cut out a bow and stick it in place.

e) Glue one edge to make a cone.

f) Thread.

4. Slotted shapes

a) Take 2 pieces of paper 5 cm x 5 cm square.

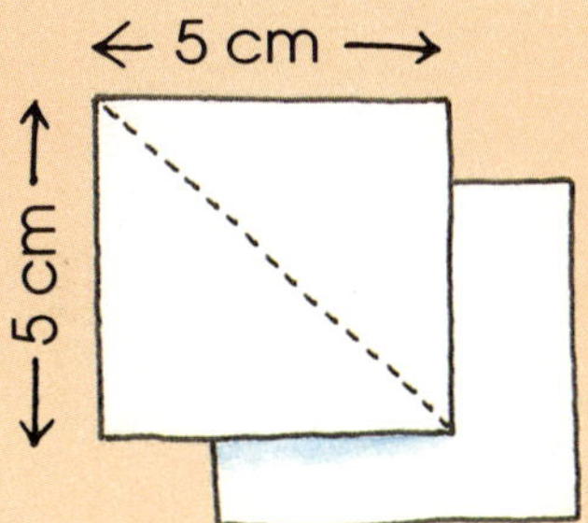

b) Make cuts to create a design.

c) Open squares out and make a slit as shown, into the centre of the square.

d) Slot the 2 pieces together and attach thread.

How to thread up your mobile.

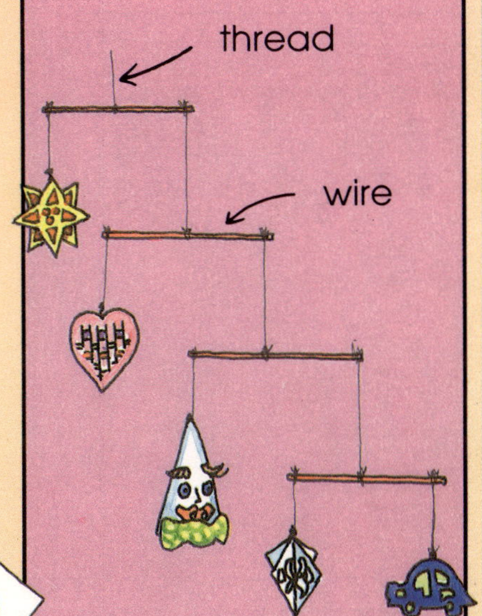

Use coated wire from florists or short lengths of cane about 20 cm long.

PAPER AND CARD

Cogs and wheels

You will need

- Corrugated card
- Cocktail sticks or used matchsticks
- Scissors
- PVA glue
- Base card - 30 cm x 20 cm approximately

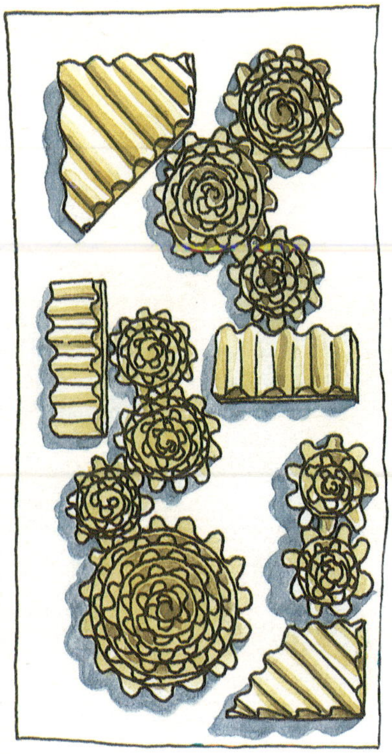

Corrugated card can be used in many ways. You can have great fun creating your own mechanical model and possibly make a marble travel across your board.

1. Cut up the corrugated card into lengths of approximately 30 cm, and of varying widths from 2 cm to 5 cm.
2. With the flat surface inside roll up the strips to make wheels.
3. Glue end to hold firm and glue a cocktail stick in the centre.

4. When you have made several wheels, arrange them on your base card and glue them in place. Pierce card with cocktail stick if you want the wheels to turn round. If you put them close together and connecting, you can make a 'working' collage. It's fun to see the direction your wheels are made to move - was it as you expected?

Add shapes of ordinary card that you have painted and decorated, to the spaces between your cogs. Or cut shapes from corrugated card and glue with the grooves uppermost.

Make a model van

1. Find two cocktail sticks at least 8 cm long to be your axles.
2. Cut four strips of corrugated card 1 cm x 8 cm. Coil card into wheel shape. Glue end to secure.
3. Make two rectangular boxes using template on page 12 as a guide.

You will need

- Card
- Corrugated card
- 2 cocktail sticks
- Scissors
- PVA glue
- Felt tips

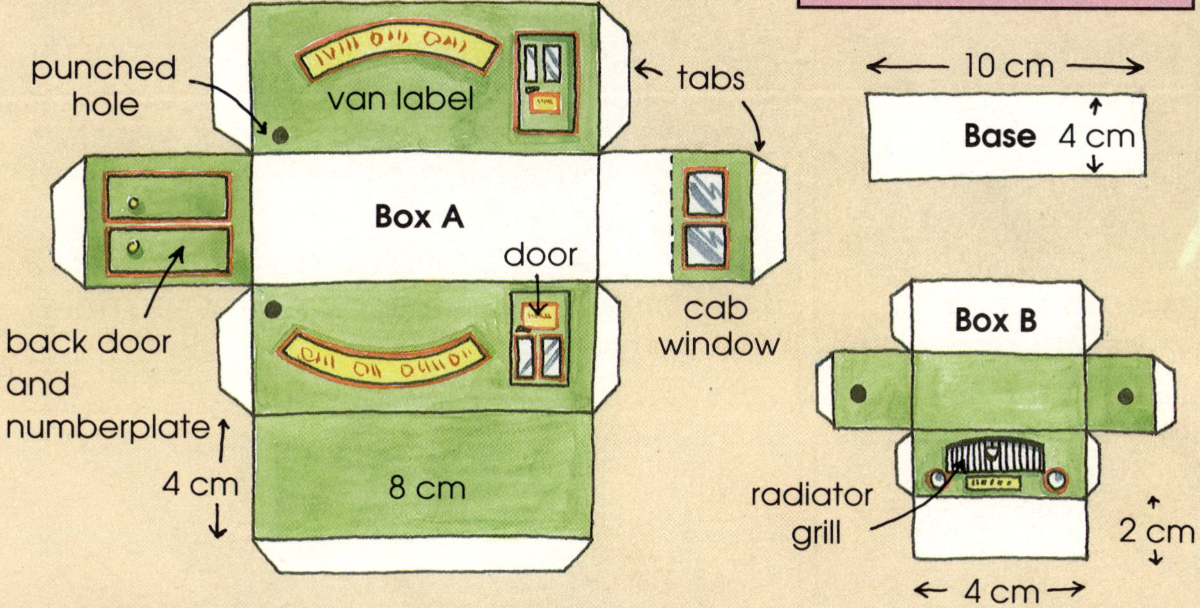

4. Score all fold lines. Fold to make boxes, but do not glue yet.
5. Punch holes where marked on plan.
6. Draw windows, doors, engine, van label, lights etc.
7. Glue tabs and stick flaps together to make boxes.
8. Stick surface B to surface A.
9. Stick to base.
10. Thread cocktail sticks through punched holes.
11. Glue four wheels on to each end of axles, but not too close to the van sides, then they will be free to turn round.

Card models: castle game

You will need

- Strong cardboard box - large brown box from a supermarket
- Craft knife
- Base card longer and wider than the box
- Various offcuts of card
- Felt tips or paints
- Marbles or tiddlywinks

It is great fun to make models of buildings. Why not make a model that you can use as a game and play with your friends? You can make up your own rules and modify the design here. You do not have to make a castle for instance, and you can vary the hazards, the number of holes and how you score. You can roll marbles or beads or use the model for a game of tiddlywinks. Follow the instructions in the diagrams to make the game.

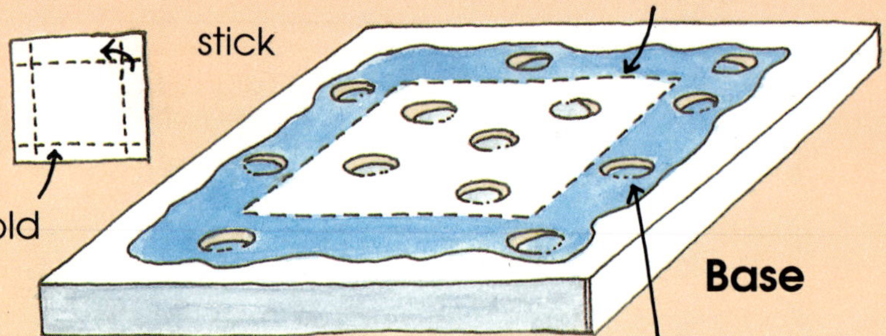

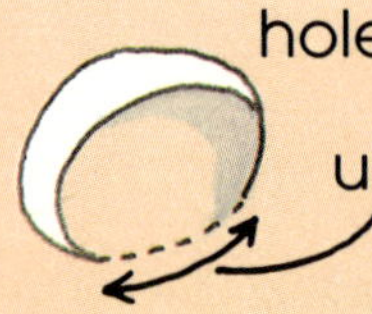

Base board with holes cut into it. Cut circular hole but leave small section uncut - push circular flap down. Give a score for each number.

If marbles touch hazards - deduct 10 points!

Castle

Make a flagpole to stick inside castle - if a marble touches it, 10 marks are deducted.

Remove base and lid from box (use spare card for hazards).

Cut castellated edge.

Holes in moat - if a marble (or tiddlywink) goes down deduct 10 points!

Cut doorway - stick door shape on to base card. This acts as a hazard.

Paint and colour your model to make it more realistic. Paint water for a moat on base board.

If playing tiddlywinks make several rings (big enough to hold the counters) with corrugated card and stick inside castle on base board. Give a score number.

PAPER AND CARD

Card dolls and puppets

You will need

- Card for doll's body
- Assortment of papers of different colours, textures and patterns
- Scissors
- 14 paper fasteners (for puppet)
- Pencil
- Felt tips

It is fun to make a card doll or puppet and create and design clothes in your chosen style. Use a variety of papers when designing their clothes, for example old wallpaper, tissue, doilies, glossy magazines, patterned wrapping paper. How inventive can you be?

For the doll

1. Draw the basic doll-shape on a piece of card.
2. Cut it out.
3. Draw on the eyes, nose and mouth.
4. Add pieces of wool, fringed or curled paper to the head to make hair.

zig-zag fold paper for a skirt

Use patterned wrapping paper for trousers.

use paper doilies for lace collars and cuffs

For the puppet

1. Draw the basic puppet-shape on to a piece of card.
2. Cut out each piece of the puppet's body.
3. Join the pieces of the puppet together with paper fasteners.
4. Draw on the eyes, nose and mouth.
5. For hair, stick on pieces of thick wool; or curl and fringe coloured paper.

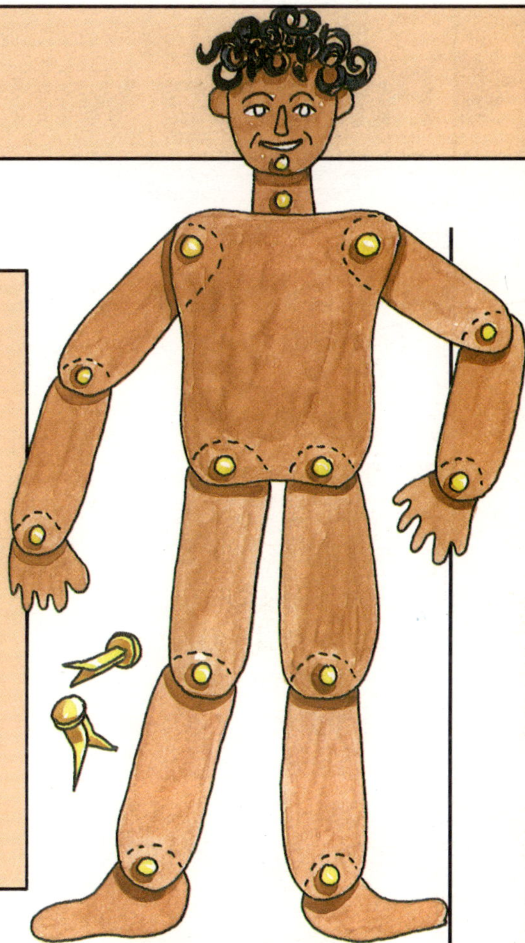

Ideas for dressing your doll or puppet

Use white tissue paper or kitchen roll for a shirt

use glossy coloured magazines for more effective costumes

handkerchiefs and scarves can be made from coloured cellophane

use coloured paper drinking straw (flattened) for tie

buttons - the discs from a paper-hole puncher

use corrugated card for corduroy effect trousers

PAPER AND CARD

Printing with card

You will need

- Various thicknesses of card, including card from brown boxes, cereal-packet card
- Paper - screwed and scrunched up into a ball
- Thick paint or printing ink - one colour only needed - in a polystyrene meat tray or plate (a piece of sponge in the plate makes a good pad)
- Large sheets of paper to print on

paint sponge

plate or meat tray

You can make very interesting prints using card in two ways, either by using the edge of interesting textured card such as corrugated card, or by building up layers of card on a base.

Printing with the edge of card

Experiment with your card, dipping the edge into the paint and testing the effects you get.

thick card bent card

cut a rough edge

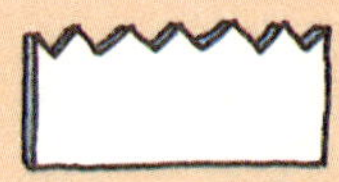

clip to make a circle

This will either produce dots or you can drag the paint - resulting in parallel lines.

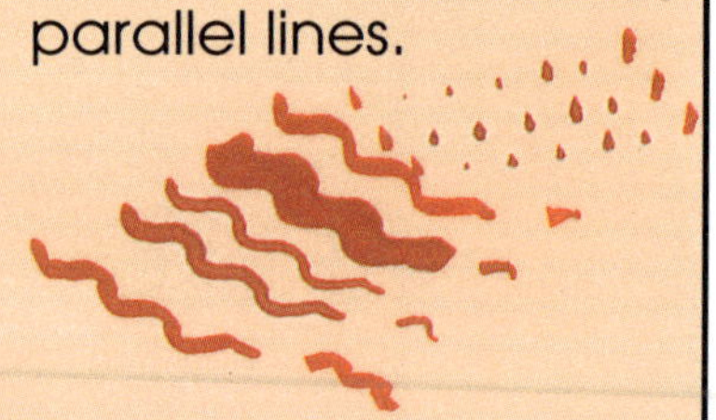

screwed-up paper

corrugated card

With ideas from your experiments, design a scene. For instance the corrugated card makes an interesting mark for roof tiles. The circles make good wheels. The serrated card makes good furrow lines for fields.

Printing with layers of card

1. Cut out required shapes and stick on to a base card about 15 cm square.
2. Various shapes can be built up in layers making contour lines.

3. Coat with paint using brush held horizontally to the card. For the best results use a roller to apply colour.
4. Print on to sheet of paper, pressing firmly with fingers or by using a dry, clean roller (a rolling pin will do).

You will need

- Offcuts of card
- Paper to print on
- Paint or printing ink in a tray
- Scissors
- PVA glue
- Large brush or roller

More ideas

Place a piece of paper over your card block and take a rubbing using a wax crayon.

PAPER AND CARD

Notes for parents and teachers

Books to read

POPULAR GUIDE TO PAPER CRAFTS
by Alan and Gill Bridgewater (Argus Books, 1987)
PAPER PLEASURES
by Faith Shannon (Mitchell Beazley, 1988)
ORIGAMI AND PAPER CRAFT
by Paul Jackson and Vivien Frank (Apple Press, 1988)
INSTANT PAPER TOYS - TO POP, SPIN, WHIRL AND FLY and QUICK AND EASY PAPER TOYS
by Richard Churchill (Blandford Press, 1987)
ORIGAMI FOR PARTIES
by Kazuo Kobayashi (Kodansha Luter International, 1987)
PAPERCRAFT PROJECTS WITH ONE PIECE OF PAPER
by Michael Grater (Dover, 1987)

Too often it is thought that paper is only for writing or drawing on. But it is a very versatile medium.

You can help children to become involved in the projects outlined in this book by encouraging them to collect all kinds of papers and card.

Papers have different textures and weights; they come in varying thicknesses; they can be matt or glossy or transparent. Some papers fold better than others, and some tear more easily than others. Paper does not always have to be cut. Torn edges add a dimension when you curl paper, overlap shapes or when incorporated in a large piece of paper weaving.

Encourage children to experiment when trying out the different techniques, by using several different papers, or by combining them within the one project.

Many of the projects suggested in this book can be extended into the classroom situation. For example, can the children find ways of expressing the surface texture of an object by selecting whether to curl or tear, cut, pleat or crinkle paper?

There are several techniques and activities that have not been included. A range of work can be done in COLLAGE - using different types of paper children can cut regular shapes or discover what happens when different papers are torn. Incidentally, by virtue of the manufacturing process there is a grain to paper. Let children tear newspaper lengthwise and crosswise to see which direction tears most effectively and easily.

Paper stiffened with PVA is an admirable material for MODELLING, not only on a small scale such as puppet heads, but for larger models of figures or animals or for creating large pictures in relief. Bowls and boxes can also be made by MOULDING paper pulp. Overlapping strips of stretched tissue paper creates an interesting surface cover.

There are many techniques for DECORATING paper - splattering with paint; various printing methods; marbling; spraying; crinkling and creasing before spraying.

Decorated papers and card can be used in PACKAGING and as COVERS for books, thus linking work with other areas of the curriculum - books that contain the children's own stories, poems and project work. A link with mathematics is made when designing nets for different kinds of packages.

In the making of paper, incorporate vegetables and grasses, plants and tiny pieces of fabric (anything fibrous) to create different patterns and textures. Testing for colour and texture and strength becomes a scientific process.

Glossary

Axle A rod that goes through the centre of wheels to join them to something.
Castellated Having turrets and battlements like a castle.
Cogs The 'teeth' on the edge of a gearwheel.
Dimensions The measurements of the size of an object - the length, width and height.
Fibrous Made up of many fibres or pieces of material such as wood.
Gauze Any thin open-work material, such as netting or wire.
Hazards Obstacles in a game that a player has to get over or around so as not to lose points.
Pulp A wet mixture of fibres from which paper is made.
Scoring Making a crease line on paper or card either by using the back of a blade or a pair of scissors. Only cut partway through card with a blade. This ensures a neat and accurate fold line.
Template A pattern used to help shape something accurately.

Index